Daily Readings with
St Teresa of Avila

Dear Kathy!
Happy Birthday!
Love ya, hon —
Pat & Pat

Daily Readings with St Teresa of Avila

Introduced and edited by

Sister Mary ODC

FOREWORD BY RUTH BURROWS

Templegate Publishers/Springfield, Illinois

First published in 1985 by
Darton, Longman and Todd Ltd
89 Lillie Road, London SW6 1UD

ISBN 0-87243-146-0

First published in the United States in 1986 by
Templegate Publishers
302 E. Adams St./P.O. Box 5152
Springfield, Illinois 62705

Remember our Lord invited 'all'. He is truth itself; His word cannot be doubted. His mercy is so great that He prevents no one from coming to this fountain of life to drink of it.

St Teresa *Way of Perfection* 19:20

Contents

Foreword

St Teresa once explained herself as a woman so deeply in love that there was not a moment when she was not occupied with her beloved, be it thinking of him, speaking to him, working for him, talking or writing about him. Perhaps her greatest gift to the Church is not what she did or the particular things she wrote but simply the witness of a woman for whom God was an overriding passion.

And this reveals to us that God is such that he can be loved like that: that he is real, living, personal; that Jesus can become the beloved of a human heart. Is there any greater incentive to faith than contact with someone of burning faith: any greater support in darkness than the shining certitude of one who really knows him?

This selection of St Teresa's writings culled by one very familiar with them contains many luminous sayings, much practical advice, but perhaps what matters most is that they bring us close to one who lived 'as seeing him who is invisible' (Heb.11:27).

RUTH BURROWS

Introduction

St Teresa of Jesus wrote four major works: her autobiography, *The Way of Perfection, The Interior Castle* and *The Foudations*. The passages in this book are largely from the first two books.

THE LIFE OF ST TERESA OF JESUS

In every autobiography there is a theme: if the author is a sportsman then it is likely that there will be details of early prowess with ball, javelin, hurdles or anything similar: this interest dominates the whole book; relationships, travel, growing up, every life experience is set within the context of this passion for sport. It is the same with any other interest: an explorer concentrates on early aptitudes for discovery, a scientist with the various youthful experiments he conducted. St Teresa is no exception to this general rule.

St Teresa was a pray-er. Her account of her life is continually interrupted by long digressions on prayer. She recounts the struggles she had with recollection, with her own vanity and desires for worldly pleasures. She minimizes nothing. The picture she draws of a woman caught between her passion for the things of this world and an equal passion for God is very real, and very encouraging to her readers. After twenty years she surrendered totally to God and her life's journey is seen to be a journey into intimate union with God. The road she travelled was that of prayer.

THE WAY OF PERFECTION

This book was originally written for Carmelites, but it is a manual of prayer for everyone. The first part speaks of the necessity of acquiring virtue if we would be truly contemplative: a proper attitude towards created things, the abandonment of self-esteem and excessive care for oneself, and an unselfish love of our neighbour. These are the external signs of true prayer and St Teresa expects to find them in Carmelites. The second part is a commentary on the Our Father. This deals with one phrase at a time and in so doing covers the whole spiritual journey.

Later in this introduction mention will be made of the most important aspects of her teaching on prayer, but we might note here that it is all extremely practical: there is nothing theoretical or abstract about it. It is concerned with the reality of everyday life. St Teresa points out again and again that daily life is the place where the authenticity of prayer is proved. Prayer must reveal itself in our actions.

HER LIFE

St Teresa was born on 28 March 1515. Her twenty-year-old mother was the second wife of Don Alonso Sanchez de Cepeda. Teresa had a stepbrother and stepsister, and her own mother bore seven sons and two daughters in rapid succession. Exhausted with so much child-bearing she died in 1528.

There are several well-known episodes from Teresa's early years which are indicative of her

10

later characteristics when a mature woman. The first of these is best recounted in her own words:

> My brother and I used to read the Lives of the Saints together. When I read of martyrdom undergone by the Saints for the love of God, it struck me that the vision of God was very cheaply purchased . . . I used to discuss with my brother how we could become martyrs. We settled to go together to the country of the Moors, begging our way for the love of God, that we might be there beheaded; and our Lord, I believe, had given us courage enough, even at so tender an age, if we could have found the means to proceed; but our greatest difficulty seemed to be our father and mother. (*Life* 1:4)

In fact she persuaded her brother to accompany her, but their flight was discovered and they were brought back, Teresa having to bear the blame. Here we see her capacity to determine on a course of action and carry it through, at whatever cost, as well as her power of persuasion. As the enterprise was undertaken as a means to purchase the vision of God, one could say that she had early established her priorities, but they were to be assailed by many lesser desires as she grew through her teens.

A second feature of her childhood was the result of this frustration of her attempt to die a martyr. She persuaded her brother to help her build hermitages in the garden. It seems to have been rather more serious than just child's play: 'I contrived to be alone, for the sake of saying my prayers . . . I used to delight . . . in the building of monasteries,

11

as if we were nuns: I gave alms as I could' (*Life*
1:6).

The thought of pain or happiness lasting
throughout eternity made a deep impression on
Teresa and she would often repeat: 'For ever and
ever'. Reflecting on the fact of everlasting life
played a large part in her initial decision to become
a nun.

One of the legacies from her mother was an
enjoyment of the contemporary tales of chivalry
with their strongly romantic nature. The lover is
joined to the loved one after terrible and fright-
ening dangers: the fidelity of both has been tried
in the fire of battle, or disaster, thus enriching
the final union. As this was the period of Spain's
exploration into the New World, and many of her
brothers were involved in expeditions, these tales
of adventure in strange lands attracted her as they
did many of her contemporaries. They fed her
emotions and confronted her with a choice of love
for the things of this world, seen simply as good
in themselves, or for the things of God, from
whom flow the good things of this world. Was
the context of her life to be merely earth, or earth
as the way of pilgrimage to heaven?

Her resoluteness, her charm and persuasive
nature, her convictions about eternity as deter-
mining the choices of life, her longing for love to
be the mainspring of life, and her struggle to put
her own passionate nature totally at the disposal
of him who is Love itself, all these factors recur
throughout her later life. She was growing up in
a period of history colourful and dramatic in every
way: Luther was challenging established Catholic

tradition; scholars were entering new fields of thought; trade was ranging further afield; it was as though the world's boundaries were being extended in every area of life.

As an adolescent Teresa was a vivacious and attractive young woman, subject to all the normal allurements of a frivolous life and at least one friendship for which she later reproached herself. Her stepsister had taken her mother's place and supervised Teresa's life but, when she herself was planning to marry, this surveillance became less attentive. Teresa was more easily exposed to a variety of personal influences, and later wrote of this: 'I am amazed at the evil one bad companion can do: the conversation of this person so changed me that no trace was left of my soul's natural disposition to virtue' (*Life* 2:5).

Staying with an uncle during a period of convalescence she read many of his books and came to understand 'that all things are as nothing, the world vanity, and rapidly passing away'. She decided that the religious state was the safest and 'resolved to force myself into it'. Her father would not consent so she ran away, yet again. At this stage it was not love of God that was driving her on but concern for her salvation. Her great love for her father made leaving home so acutely painful that 'it seemed to me as if every bone in my body were being wrenched asunder' (*Life* 4:1).

She entered the Convent of the Incarnation, Avila, in 1536 and the following year fell seriously ill. There was a time in 1538 when Teresa was considered dead and all preparations were made for her funeral. However, after four days of being

13

unconscious, she 'came to herself' and slowly regained her health.

She was full of gratitude and good resolutions about prayer, resolutions which she did not keep as is revealed in these words: 'Once, O Lord, I thought it impossible to forsake Thee so utterly; and now that I have forsaken Thee so often, I cannot help being afraid'; yet she adds: 'Though I have forsaken Thee, Thou hast not forsaken me so utterly but that Thou hast come again and raised me up, giving me Thy hand always. Very often, O Lord, I would not take it; very often I would not listen when Thou wert calling me again' (*Life* 6:16).

Her life oscillated between frivolity and entertaining friends in the parlour, and her deeper desires for friendship with God. However, she admits that she 'was ashamed to draw near unto God in an act of such special friendship as prayer' (*Life* 7:1). Her father's death, an encounter with a Dominican and her own self-dissatisfaction caused her to resume regular prayer. The ups and downs continued until one day a picture of our Lord in his Passion shocked her into realizing clearly that she was trifling with grace, blocking God's work in and through her and resisting his love. After this she resolved to pursue the way of prayer as diligently as she could. She consulted advisers, both Jesuits and Dominicans, always doubting her own ideas and experiences, but courageously cultivating the presence of God and seeking his companionship in her own daily life.

In 1558 St Peter of Alcántara came to Avila and was able to reassure St Teresa when many other priests were condemning her as a woman deceived by her experiences in prayer. At that time she had visions and locutions, and was only too ready to think herself deceived. She speaks of him at length in the *Life* (ch. 27), of his encouragement, his austerity and his sanctity. It is surely most telling (and equally telling for our contemporary society, which has a certain mistrust of eremitical holiness), when she comments: 'His weakness was so great, that he seemed like nothing else but the roots of trees. With all his sanctity, he was very agreeable; though his words were few, unless when asked questions, he was very pleasant to speak to, for he had a most clear understanding' (*Life* 27:19).

Teresa reflected on her own manner of serving God and on the Rule observed in her own monastery. She recognized that there was considerable laxity, and commended the matter to our Lord in prayer. As a result she felt impelled to found a house in which the Primitive Rule of the Order would be observed. She 'could not doubt that our Lord wanted this' and persevered in the plans for its establishment despite opposition.

FOUNDATIONS

On 24 August 1562 the first house of the Reform, St Joseph's, was founded. It was supported by St Peter of Alcántara, but opposed by many of the local people and by many of her own community who felt that she was an upstart who was criticizing their own life-style by this action. 'It was said I insulted my sisters.' Over the next twenty

15

years she founded fifteen more houses for the Discalced[1] Carmelite nuns and, in association with St John of the Cross, at least two for the friars.

The foundations were made at the order of the Father General, and are recounted in detail in the Book of the Foundations. They are a remarkable achievement considering the nature of transport in those days – usually closed-in waggons – and the climate. It was either suffocatingly hot, or fiercely cold. The inns were often dirty, the food bad and the attitude of the clergy varied from one extreme to the other. As for the general populace, the nuns were a source of curiosity and often of ridicule. Throughout her travels St Teresa carried an hourglass with her so that the hours of the Office and of silent prayer might be observed. Her energy, resolution and sense of humour were unfailing, animated as they were by her desire to serve her Lord as lovingly as she could.

St Teresa died at Alba de Tormes on 4 October 1582. That evening she received communion, knowing it to be her Viaticum, and exclaimed: 'O my Bridegroom, at last the longed-for hour has come! Now it is time for us to see one another! Blessed be this hour, and may Thy will be done!' With her daughters kneeling and praying beside her Teresa asked their forgiveness and repeated these words of the psalm: 'A humble and contrite heart, O Lord, Thou wilt not despise.' Shortly

[1] Discalced meaning literally 'unshod' distinguishes Teresa's foundations from the earlier Calced congregations. More comprehensively, the word indicates the stricter ascetic discipline of the reformed foundations.

after murmuring the name of Jesus she became unable to speak and died in the arms of her devoted and well-loved infirmarian, Sister Anne of St Bartholomew. The Requiem and burial took place at Alba the next day.

St Teresa was sixty-seven years old, having spent twenty-six years as a nun in the convent of the Incarnation at Avila, and another twenty years as foundress of the Discalced Carmelites. When the bells of Avila tolled for her, the local citizens said: 'The Saint has gone to heaven.'

This brief sketch of St Teresa's life has omitted many details of persecutions and trials, both within the Order and from outside, by clergy, religious and laity, but it shows that Teresa de Ahumada y Cepeda was not born a saint: she became one, by struggling to respond, first by sheer will-power and then by a desire to return love for Love, to her Lord and God.

As a result of Gregory XIII's reform of the calendar, her feast is kept on 15 October, not on 4 October.

There is no more fitting epitaph for her than her own poem, 'St Teresa's Bookmark':

> Let nothing disturb thee,
> Nothing affright thee;
> All things are passing;
> God never changeth;
> Patient endurance
> Attaineth to all things;
> Who God possesseth
> In nothing is wanting;
> Alone God sufficeth.

17

THE RELEVANCE OF TERESA'S SPIRITUAL WAY TO OUR CONTEMPORARY WORLD

Today there is much talk of personal relationships. To Teresa these were vital – literally – her source of life. That was true in an absolute sense of her relationship to Christ. When she realized that he was the only way to the Father she tried to get to know him by every means in her power: through scripture, hearing good sermons, talking with priests and others renowned for their spiritual learning, and above all by reflecting on his life and message. Just as one advances in knowledge and love of another human being with whom one lives, so did Teresa with her Lord and Friend, Jesus. She shared all with him, whose human life and sufferings she saw reflected in her own.

Teresa carried this sharing into the concrete situations of everyday life. She shared *everything* with Christ, both happy and unhappy events. Any failure in virtue or other form of unloving she would see as material to be laid on the altar just as much as generous unselfish actions. The former need not be a stumbling block if faced and accepted: they can be converted by trust and effort into springboards for personal change. Thus her approach was always positive: everything was fuel for the fire of the love of God.

Her letters lead the recipients towards Christ, to seek strength or guidance by prayer. She writes to Maria de Mendoza (26 March 1578): 'He will not fail to console you in this sorrow and to recall to your memory what His Majesty and His

18

glorious Mother suffered in this holy season. If we realize this as we ought, we shall bear all life's trials easily. I should like to be with you so as to share your grief.' To Mother Mary of St Joseph (22 July 1579) she again refers to the Passion: 'Were we to choose the trials we wanted and set aside the rest, we should not be imitating our Bridegroom, Who, keenly as He felt the ordeal of His Passion, ended His prayer in the garden . . . Fiat voluntas tua.'

Teresa tested the authenticity of prayer by its fruits. Human life is a whole, and our real values are revealed in the choices we make and in our behaviour. It is useless to make fine resolutions or to have beautiful thoughts if we remain selfish in daily living.

Relationships with others are the touchstone of our progress in prayer. 'What value God places on our loving and keeping peace with one another! The good Jesus places it before anything else' (*Way* 36:6).

How forgetful of her ease, how unmindful of honours and how far from seeking men's esteem should she be whose soul God thus chooses for His special dwelling-place! For if her mind is fixed on Him as it ought to be, she must needs forget herself: all her thoughts are bent on how to please Him better, and when and how she can show the love she bears Him. . . . It will do me little good to be deeply recollected when alone, making acts of the virtues, planning and promising to do wonders

19

in God's service, if, afterwards, when occasion offers, I do just the opposite. (*IC* 7:4,9,10)

Teresa fostered her friendship with Christ by every means in her power, setting aside anything that did not advance her purpose of getting to know Christ her Lord better. Her enthusiasm was relentless, but her resolution was cheerful. She had no use for 'sour-faced saints'.

Two sentences at the end of *The Interior Castle* (7:4,23) sum up her teaching: 'Our Lord does not care so much for the importance of our works as for the love with which they are done. When we do all we can, His Majesty will enable us to do more every day.'

SISTER MARY ODC
Carmelite Monastery
Quidenham
Norwich

Prayer

Is A Great
Blessing

Prayer is a great blessing

How great is the good which God works in a soul when He gives it a disposition to pray in earnest, though it may not be so well prepared as it ought to be.

If that soul perseveres in spite of sins, temptations and relapses, brought about in a thousand ways by Satan, our Lord will bring it at last – I am certain of it – to the harbour of salvation, as He has brought me myself.

May His Majesty grant I may never go back and be lost!

He who gives himself to prayer is in possession of a great blessing, of which many saintly men have written – I am speaking of mental prayer – glory be to God for it!

Let him never cease from prayer who has once begun it, be his life ever so wicked; for prayer is the way to amend it, and without prayer such amendment will be much more difficult.

As to him who has not begun to pray, I implore him by the love of our Lord not to deprive himself of so great a good.

Take God as your Friend

 In prayer there is nothing to be afraid of, but everything to hope for. Granting that someone does not advance, nor make an effort to become perfect, yet little by little he will attain to a knowledge of the road that leads to heaven.

If he perseveres, I hope in the mercy of God for him, seeing that no one ever took Him for his Friend that was not amply rewarded; for mental prayer is nothing else, in my opinion, but being on terms of friendship with God, frequently conversing in secret with Him Who, we know, loves us.

O Life of all lives, Thou slayest none that put their trust in Thee, and seek Thy friendship; yea, rather, Thou sustainest their bodily life in greater vigour, and makest their soul to live.

Prayer is the door

Prayer is the door to those great graces which our Lord bestowed upon me.

If this door be shut, I do not see how He can bestow them; for even if He entered into a soul to take His delight therein, and to make that soul also delight in Him, there is no way by which He can do so; for His will is, that such a soul should be lonely and pure, with a great desire to receive His graces.

If we put many hindrances in the way, and take no pains whatever to remove them, how can He come to us, and how can we have any desire that He should show us His great mercies?

Above all I implore all for the love of our Lord, and for the great love with which He goeth about seeking our conversion to Himself, to beware of the occasions of sin: for once placed therein, we have no ground to rest on.

Why persevere in prayer?

It is essential to begin the practice of prayer with a firm resolution of persevering in it.

When we pay this attention of our thoughts – an attention which is not without profit but which brings us a rich reward – when we render this homage to God, Who has bestowed so much on us and Who continues to shower benefits upon us, it would be wrong not to give it Him entirely; not as one who gives a thing meaning to take it back again. This cannot be called 'giving'.

Where can a wife be found who, after receiving a number of valuable jewels from her husband, will not give him in return even a ring, not so much for its value (for all she possesses is his) but as a pledge that she will be faithful to him unto death?

Since we have resolved to devote to God this short space of time (which we should otherwise bestow on ourselves or our friends who would not thank us for it) let us yield it Him with thoughts that are free and withdrawn from all else.

Let us fully resolve never to take it back, whatever crosses it may bring us, and in spite of all aridities.

Prayer and the Bridegroom

Before prayer, endeavour to realize Whose Presence you are approaching and to Whom you are about to speak, keeping in mind Whom you are addressing.

If our lives were a thousand times as long as they are we should never fully understand how we ought to behave towards God, before Whom the angels tremble, Who *can* do all He wills, and with Whom to wish is to accomplish. Ought we not, my daughters, to rejoice in these perfections of our Bridegroom, and to learn to know Him and what our lives should be?

God bless me! When a girl is going to be married she knows who her husband is to be and what are his means and position, shall not we think about our Bridegroom before He takes us home on the wedding-day?

Why should I be prevented from understanding Who this Man is, Who is His Father, to what country He will take me, what are the riches He promises to endow me with, and what rank He holds? May I not know how best to please Him, what are His tastes, and how to bring my mind to harmonize with His?

To understand these truths is to practise mental prayer.

Keep close to the Lord

Let us return to consider our vocal prayer, in order to pray intelligently, and in such a way that, without our understanding how, God may give us all the rest.

As you are alone, seek for some companion – and where could you find a better one than the Master Who taught you the prayer you are about to say?

Picture this same Lord close beside you. See how lovingly, how humbly He is teaching you – believe me, you should never be without so good a Friend.

If you accustom yourselves to draw Him near you, and He sees that you love to have Him and make every effort to please Him, you will be unable, so to speak, to send Him away.

He will never fail you, but will help you in all your troubles and you will find Him everywhere.

Do you think it is a small thing to have such a Friend at your side?

A garden for the Lord

 A beginner must look upon himself as making a garden, wherein our Lord may take His delight, but in a soil unfruitful, and abounding in weeds.

His Majesty roots up the weeds, and sets good plants in their place.

Let us take for granted that this is already done when a soul is determined to give itself to prayer, and has begun the practice of it.

We have then, as good gardeners, by the help of God to see that the plants grow, to water them carefully, that they may not die, but produce blossoms, which shall send forth much fragrance, refreshing to our Lord, so that He may come often for His pleasure into this garden, and delight Himself in the midst of these virtues.

Watering the garden

Let us see how this garden is to be watered, that we may understand what we have to do: how much trouble it will cost us, whether the gain be greater than the trouble, or how long it will take us.

It seems to me that the garden may be watered in four ways: by water taken out of a well, which is very laborious; or with water raised by a water-wheel and buckets, drawn by a windlass – I have drawn it this way sometimes – it is a less trouble-some way than the first, and gives more water; or by a stream or brook, whereby the garden is watered in a much better way – for the soil is more thoroughly saturated, and there is no necessity to water it so often, and the labour of the gardener is much less; or by showers of rain, when our Lord Himself waters it, without labour on our part – and this way is incomparably better than all the others of which I have spoken.

I hope by the help of this comparison, to explain the four degrees of prayer to which our Lord, of His goodness, has occasionally raised my soul.

Beginning

Of those who are beginners in prayer, we may say that they are those who draw the water up out of the well – a process which, as I have said, is very laborious; for they must be wearied in keeping the senses recollected, and this is a great labour, because the senses have been hitherto accustomed to distractions.

It is necessary for beginners to accustom themselves to disregard what they hear or see, and to put it away from them during the time of prayer; they must be alone, and in retirement think over their past life.

Beginners at first suffer much, because they are not convinced that they are penitent for their sins; and yet they are, because they are so sincerely resolved on serving God.

They must strive to meditate on the life of Christ, and the understanding is wearied thereby.

Thus far we can advance of ourselves – that is, by the grace of God – for without that, as every one knows, we never can have one good thought.

With the Lord as Friend

 With so good a Friend and Captain ever present, Himself the first to suffer, everything can be borne.

He helps, He strengthens, He never fails, He is the true Friend.

I see clearly, and since then have always seen, that if we are to please God, and if He is to give us His great graces, everything must pass through the hands of His most sacred humanity, in whom His Majesty said that He is well pleased.

I know this by repeated experience: I have seen clearly that this is the door by which we are to enter, if we would have His supreme Majesty reveal to us His great secrets.

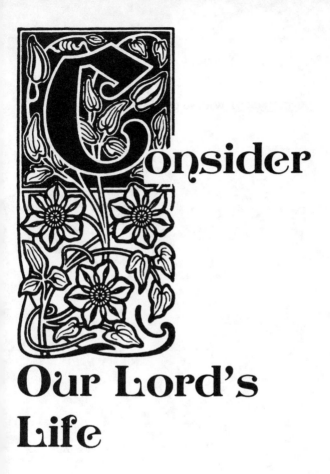

Consider

Our Lord's Life

Consider our Lord's life

Our Lord is He by whom all good things come to us; He will teach you.

Consider His life; that is the best example.

What more can we want than so good a Friend at our side, Who will not forsake us when we are in trouble and distress, as they do who belong to the world!

Blessed is he who truly loves Him, and who always has Him near him!

Let us consider the glorious St Paul, who seems as if Jesus was never absent from his lips, as if he had Him deep down in his heart.

After I had heard this of some great saints given to contemplation, I considered the matter carefully; I see they walked in no other way. St Francis with the stigmata proves it, St Anthony of Padua with the Infant Jesus; St Bernard rejoiced in the sacred humanity; so did St Catherine of Siena and many others.

See yourself in Him

If you feel happy, think of Our Lord at His Resurrection, for the very thought of how He rose from the tomb will delight you. How He shone with splendour! What spoils He brought away from the battle, where He won a glorious kingdom that He wishes to make all your own and Himself with it. Is it much to look but once on Him Who gives you such riches?

If you have trials to bear, if you are sorrowful, watch Him on His way to the garden. What grief must have arisen in His soul to cause Him, who was patience itself, to manifest and complain of it!

Or see Him bound to the column, full of sufferings, His flesh all torn to pieces because of His tender love for you.

Or look on Him laden with the cross, and not allowed to stay to take breath.

He will gaze on you with beautiful, compassionate eyes, and will forget His own grief to solace yours, only because you went to comfort Him, and turned to look at Him.

We cannot speak to God and the world at the same time

You know that His Majesty taught us that the first point is that prayer should be made in solitude.

He practised this Himself; not because it was requisite for Him, but for the sake of our instruction. I have already explained that we cannot speak both to God and to the world at the same time.

Yet what else are we doing if, while we pray, we listen to other people's conversation or let our thoughts dwell unchecked on whatever subject occurs to them?

On other occasions God permits a tempest of difficulties to assault His servants for His greater gain: then, though the soul may grieve at its distractions and try to stop them, this is found to be impossible. She should not trouble herself about it; this would only increase the evil.

Let her pray as best she can, or leave off praying and rest her soul as if she were ill, occupying herself with some other good work.

Second degree of prayer

Let us now speak of the second manner of drawing water, which the Lord of the vineyard has ordained; of the machine of wheel and buckets whereby the gardener may draw more water with less labour, and be able to take some rest without being continually at work. I apply this to the prayer called the prayer of quiet.

Herein the soul begins to be recollected; it is now touching on the supernatural – for it never could by any efforts of its own attain to this.

This is a gathering together of the faculties of the soul within itself, but the faculties are not lost, neither are they asleep; the will alone is occupied in such a way that, without knowing how it has become a captive, it gives a simple consent to become the prisoner of God; for it knows well what it is to be the captive of Him it loves.

O my Jesus and my Lord, how pressing now is Thy love! It binds our love in bonds so straitly, that it is not in its power at this moment to love anything else but Thee.

A spark of true love

The prayer of quiet, then, is a little spark of the true love of Himself, which our Lord begins to enkindle in the soul; and His will is that the soul should understand what this love is by the joy it brings.

This spark given of God, however slight it may be, causes a great crackling; if men do not quench it by their faults, it is the beginning of a great fire, which sends forth the flames of that most vehement love of God which His Majesty will have perfect souls possess.

What the soul has to do is nothing more than to be gentle and without noise. By noise, I mean going about with the understanding in search of words and reflections whereby to give God thanks for His grace, and heaping up its sins and imperfections together to show that it does not deserve it.

Let it simply say words of love that suggest themselves now, firmly grounded in the conviction that what it says is truth.

We need to anchor our thoughts

 We are not angels, for we have a body; to seek to make ourselves angels while we are on the earth, and so much on the earth as I was, is an act of folly.

In general, our thoughts must have something to rest on, though the soul may go forth out of itself now and then, or it may be very often so full of God as to be in need of no created thing by the help of which it may recollect itself. But this is not so common.

When we have many things to do, when we are persecuted and in trouble, when we cannot have much rest, and when we have our seasons of dryness, Christ is our best Friend; for we regard Him as Man, and behold Him faint and in trouble. and He is our Companion.

When we have accustomed ourselves in this way, it is very easy to find Him near us, although there will be occasions from time to time when we can do neither the one nor the other.

Look at Him

I am not asking you to make many reflections, to produce grand and subtle considerations with your intellect, or to feel deep devotion: I only ask you to look at Him.

Who can prevent your turning the eyes of your soul (but for an instant, if you can do no more) on our Lord? You are able to look on many ugly things: then can you not gaze upon the fairest sight imaginable? Your Bridegroom never takes His eyes off you!

He has borne with many offences and much unworthiness in you, yet these have not sufficed to make Him turn away: is it much to ask that you should sometimes shift your gaze from earthly things to fix it on Him?

You will find that He suits Himself to whatever mood you are in. He longs so keenly for our glance that He will neglect no means to win it.

Let us go together, Lord

St Teresa prays: 'If it be Thy will to suffer thus for me, what do I suffer for Thee in return? Let us go together, Lord: "whither Thou goest, I will go", and I will follow where Thou hast passed.'

Take no notice of what is said to you; shut your ears to all murmurings; stumble and fall with your Bridegroom, but do not draw back from the cross nor abandon it.

Often recall His weariness and how much harder His labours were than your own, however great you may fancy these to be and whatever pain they cause you.

What must have been the sufferings of the glorious Virgin and the Magdalene! What threats, what evil words, what insolence, what shocks!

Do not imagine that you would have endured these heavy trials if you cannot bear the light ones you meet with now: practise patience with these, and you may receive greater crosses later on.

Coax your own soul to be still

It is an aid to read a good devotional book in the vernacular, in order to learn how to collect the thoughts and to pray well vocally, thus, little by little, enticing the soul by coaxing and persuasion, so that it may not take alarm.

Be wary, for it deserted its Bridegroom many years ago, and needs very careful management to induce it to return to its home.

We sinners have so accustomed ourselves and our thoughts to run after pleasure (or pain, as it might be more fitly called), that the poor soul no longer understands itself, and needs many stratagems to make it stay at home with its Spouse, yet unless we succeed in doing this we shall accomplish nothing.

Keep close to this kind Master, firmly resolved to learn all He teaches you. He will ensure your proving good scholars, and will never leave you unless you first desert Him.

Attend to His words and you will realize what love He bears you: it is no small gain and joy to feel sure of the Tutor's affection.

Humility is the foundation of prayer

 God is greatly pleased when He beholds a soul in its humility making His Son a Mediator between itself and Him, and yet loving Him so much as to confess its own unworthiness, even when He would raise it up to the highest contemplation, and saying with St Peter: 'Go away from me, O Lord, for I am a sinful man.'

I know this by experience; it was thus that God directed my soul. I have understood that the whole foundation of prayer must be laid in humility, and that the more a soul humbles itself in prayer, the more God lifts it up.

I do not remember that He ever showed me any of those marvellous mercies of which I shall speak at any other time than when I was as one brought to nothing, by seeing how wicked I was.

Moreover His Majesty contrived to make me understand matters that helped me to know myself, but which I could never have even imagined of myself.

God

Always
Wills Our
Greater
Gain

Other souls receiving no spiritual consola~~tion~~ ~~doubt whether it is~~ not through their own fault and are most anxious to improve.

When they see any one else shed a tear, unless they do the same they think they must be much more backward than she is in God's service, although perhaps they are more advanced, for tears, though good, do not always indicate perfection.

Humility, mortification, detachment, and other virtues are safest: there is no cause for fear, nor need you doubt that you may become as perfect as the greatest contemplatives.

You may be sure, if you do all you can and prepare yourselves for contemplation as I have described, that if He does not grant it to you (though I believe, if your humility and detachment are sincere, He will grant it), He is keeping back this consolation in reserve only to give it you all at once in heaven.

True vocal prayer

Let me address myself to those who can neither recollect themselves, nor concentrate their minds on mental prayer, nor can they meditate. In fact, many are terrified at the mere name of mental prayer or contemplation.

What I will advise, or I may say *teach* you, is how to pray vocally, because you ought to understand the words you utter.

When I recite, in the Credo, 'I believe', it seems to me that I ought to know and to understand what it is that 'I believe'. If I say, 'Our Father', love requires that I should know *Who* is 'our Father', and *Who* the Master who taught us this prayer, for there is an immense difference between one master and another.

If you tell me that it is enough to know this once for all and to think no more about it, you are wrong. You might as well say that it is enough to recite the prayer itself once in a lifetime.

God forbid that whenever we say this prayer we should not think of such a Master, so loving and desirous of our good.

Living water

 I call to remembrance – oh, how often! – that living water of ██████ ████ ██ ███ █████ Samaritan woman. That Gospel has a great attraction for me; and indeed, so it had even when I was a little child, though I did not understand it then as I do now.

I used to pray much to our Lord for that living water; and I had always a picture of it, representing our Lord at the well, with this inscription, 'Lord, give me this water'.

The soul is not at rest, nor can it contain itself because of the love it has: it is so saturated that it would have others drink of it, that they might help it to praise God.

Lord, give us light

What utter blindness to seek for happiness where it cannot be found. Lord, give us light! See! we need it more than did the man who was born blind, for he longed to see the light but could not, while we do not wish to see it.

O true God of mine! How hard a thing I crave of Thee! No less than that Thou shouldst love those who do not love Thee: shouldst open to those who do not knock – shouldst cure those who wish to ail, and who foster their maladies.

Thou didst declare, my Master, that Thou camest to seek sinners: these are the real sinners! Look not on our blindness, my God, but on the streams of blood shed by Thy Son for us.

Remember Lord, we are 'the work of Thy hands'; succour us by Thy goodness and mercy!

'I will give him to drink'

O compassionate and tender Sovereign of my
soul, Who dost also say: 'If anyone thirst, let him
come to Me, and I will give him to drink!' How
parched with thirst must men be who are inflamed
with covetousness for miserable earthly goods!
Urgent is their need of this water, lest they be
totally consumed.

O Life, Who givest life to all! refuse not this most
delicious water, promised by Thee to all who
desire it. Behold, I long for it, Lord; I ask for it,
I come to thee! Thou knowest how I need it, since
it is the only cure for a soul wounded by Thee.

Let there be *one*, O Lord, at least let there be *one*
who asks Thee to enlighten him, who is capable
of leading many others to the truth! I ask this
favour not for my own sake, Lord, for I do not
deserve it, but beg it for the merits of Thy Son.
Look on His wounds, and forgive us as He
forgave the men who inflicted them.

The water of union

Souls raised to this state are as oblivious of their own loss or gain as if they no longer existed.

Their one thought is to serve and please God, for, knowing His love for His creatures, they delight in leaving their own comfort and advantages to gratify Him by helping and teaching their neighbour in order that they may profit his soul. They never calculate as to whether they will lose by it themselves, but think about the welfare of others, forgetting themselves in order to please God better – and they will even lose their lives if need be, as did many of the martyrs.

These are the fruits of which the Bride cries: 'Compass me about with apples! Send me crosses, Lord! Send me persecutions!' She no longer cares for her own pleasure, but solely for pleasing God, so she delights in imitating, in some degree, that most painful life led by Christ.

He sees that the Bride is quite lost to herself, and could He bear to withhold Himself from one who wholly gives herself to Him?

Come, drink of the fountain

We must begin [prayer] by feeling no doubt that unless we allow ourselves to be defeated we are sure to succeed. This is certain, for however insignificant our conquest may be we shall come off with great gains.

Never fear that the Lord Who invites us to drink of the fountain will allow us to die of thirst.

I have said it before and I shall often repeat it, for people who have not learnt our Lord's goodness by experience, but only know of it by faith, are often discouraged.

It is a great grace to have proved for oneself the friendship and caresses He bestows on those who walk by this way of prayer, and how, as it were, He defrays all the costs.

It does not surprise me that those who have never practised it should want the security of receiving some interest. You know that we receive a hundredfold even in this life, and that our Lord said: 'Ask and you shall receive.' If you do not believe Him it would be of little use for me to wear myself out with telling you.

Unprofitable servants

I am not saying that men should not seek to be devout, nor that they should not stand with great reverence in the presence of God, but only that they are not to vex themselves if they cannot find even one good thought, for we are unprofitable servants.

We must walk in liberty on this road, committing ourselves into the hands of God. If it be His Majesty's good pleasure to raise us, we must go willingly; if not, we must serve Him in the lower offices of His house. As I have sometimes said, God is more careful of us than we are ourselves, and knows what each one of us is fit for.

Let us then pray Him always to show His mercy upon us, with a submissive spirit, yet trusting in the goodness of God.

Now that the soul is permitted to sit at the feet of Christ, let it contrive not to quit its place. Let it follow the example of the Magdalene; and when it shall be strong enough, God will lead it into the wilderness.

How the ground is prepared for this fount of water

 If the ground is well dug by troubles, persecutions, detractions and infirmities – they are few who ascend so high without this – if it be well broken up by great detachment from all self-interest, it will drink in so much water that it can hardly ever be parched again.

But if it be ground which is mere waste, and covered with thorns (as I was when I began); if the occasions of sin be not avoided; if it be an ungrateful soil, unfitted for so great a grace, it will be parched up again.

If the gardener becomes careless, and if our Lord, out of His mere goodness, will not send down rain upon it, the garden is ruined.

Thus has it been with me more than once, so that I am amazed at it. I write this for the comfort of souls which are weak, as I am, that they may never despair, nor cease to trust in the power of God; they must not be discouraged, unless they would lose themselves utterly. Tears gain everything, and one drop of water attracts another.

Fruits of this prayer

The soul remains possessed of so much courage, that if it were now hewn in pieces for God, it would be a great consolation to it.

This is the time of resolutions, of heroic determinations, of the living energy of good desires, of the beginning of hatred of the world, and of the most clear perception of its vanity.

The soul grows in humility more and more, because it sees clearly that neither for obtaining nor retaining this grace, great beyond measure, has it ever done, or been able to do, anything of itself.

It looks upon itself as most unworthy – for in a room into which the sunlight enters strongly, not a cobweb can be hid: it sees its own misery; self-conceit is so far away, that it seems it never could have had any.

It is abiding alone with the Lord: what has it to do but to love Him?

Out of Love, Jesus Gives Us His Father

Out of love, Jesus gives us His Father

O Son of God and my Lord! How is it that Thou canst give us so much with Thy first word: 'Our Father'?

Besides humbling Thyself to the dust by joining Thy petitions to our own and making Thyself the Brother of such miserable creatures as ourselves, Thou dost give us in Thy Father's name all that can be given, since Thou dost ask Him to make us His children, and Thy word cannot fail.

Since He is our Father, He must bear with us however deeply we offend Him, if like the prodigal son, we return to Him. He must pardon us; console us in our trials; maintain us in a way that becomes Him Who must needs be a better Father than any earthly parent.

More than this, He makes us brethren and co-heirs with Thee. Behold, my Lord, with Thy love and Thy humility, nothing can be an obstacle to Thee.

Blessed be Thou for ever, Lord of mine, Who dost so love to give that naught can stay Thy hand.

Heaven is within

You know that God is everywhere, which is a great truth; wherever God dwells there is heaven, and you may feel sure that all which is glorious is near His Majesty.

Remember what St Augustine tells us – I think it comes in his Meditations; how he sought God in many places and at last found the Almighty within himself. Do you consider it of slight importance for a soul given to wandering thoughts to realize this truth and to see that it has no need to go to heaven in order to speak to the eternal Father or to enjoy His company? Nor is it requisite to raise the voice to address Him, for He hears every whisper however low.

We are not forced to take wings to find Him, but have only to seek solitude and to look within ourselves.

Address Him sometimes as Father, or as Brother, or again as a Master or as your Bridegroom: sometimes in one way, sometimes in another, He will teach you what He wishes you to do.

Embarking on prayer

When the soul collects together all the faculties and enters within itself to be with God, it is called 'recollection'. Being retired within itself, the spirit can meditate on the Passion and can there picture the Son in its thoughts, and can offer Him to the Father without tiring the mind by journeying to find Him on Mount Calvary, or in the garden or at the column.

Those who are able to enclose themselves within the little heaven of their souls where dwells the Creator of heaven and earth, and who can accustom themselves not to look at anything nor to remain in any place which would preoccupy their exterior senses, may feel sure that they are travelling by an excellent way, and that they will certainly come to drink of the water from the fountain, for they will journey far in a short time.

They resemble a man who goes by sea, and who, if the wind is favourable, gets in a few days to the end of a voyage which would have taken far longer by land. These souls may be said to have already put out to sea.

Our hearts are His kingdom

Let us realize that we have within us a most
splendid palace built entirely of gold and precious
stones – in short, one that is fit for such a Lord –
and that we are partly responsible for the
condition of this building, because there is no
structure so beautiful as a soul full of pure virtues,
and the more perfect these virtues are, the more
brilliantly do the jewels shine.

Within this palace dwells the mighty King Who
has deigned to become your Father and Who is
seated on a throne of priceless value, by which I
mean your heart.

Had I understood always, as I do now, that so
great a King resided in my soul I should not have
left Him alone so often, but should have stayed
with Him sometimes and not have kept His
dwelling-place in such disorder.

He does not force our wills but only takes what
we give Him, but He does not give Himself
entirely until He sees that we yield ourselves
entirely to Him.

Membership of the kingdom

The good Jesus bids us say these words: 'Hallowed be Thy name; Thy kingdom come in us.' It is well that we should all learn what we ask for when praying for this kingdom.

His Majesty saw that, unless He enabled us to do so by giving us His kingdom here on earth, our natural defects would render us unfit either to hallow, praise, magnify, glorify, or extol the holy name of the eternal Father. Therefore the good Jesus placed the two petitions close together.

In the kingdom of heaven the soul dwells in perfect peace and feels supreme satisfaction at seeing that all those around it honour and praise God and bless His name, and at knowing that they never offend Him.

In heaven everyone loves Him; the soul cares for nothing but loving Him: it cannot cease to do so because it knows Him as He is.

If only we knew Him we should love Him in the same way in this world, and although not so constantly and so perfectly as in heaven, yet very differently from what we do now.

Like Martha

 His Majesty does not lead all souls by the same way. St Martha was holy, though we are never told she was a contemplative; would you not be content with resembling this blessed woman who deserved to receive Christ our Lord so often into her home, where she fed and served Him, and where He ate at her table?

Imagine that this little community is the house of St Martha where there must be different kinds of people. Remember that someone must cook the meals and count yourselves happy in being able to serve like Martha.

Reflect that true humility consists in being willing and ready to do what our Lord asks of us. It always makes us consider ourselves unworthy to be reckoned among His servants.

Then if contemplation, mental and vocal prayer, nursing the sick, the work of the house and the most menial labour, all serve this Guest, why should we choose to minister to Him in one way rather than in another?

Look at Him

O Lord! all our ills come from not fixing our eyes
on Thee: if we looked at nothing else but the way,
we should soon arrive, but we fall a thousand
times and stumble and go astray because we do
not keep our eyes fixed on the true way.

It seems as though we were not Christians at all,
nor had ever in our lives read the Passion. Some
slight disrespect is shown us and we at once cry
out: 'We are not saints!' So say I. God deliver us
from saying 'we are not saints' when we fall into
any imperfection.

Let there be nothing which we know would
further our Lord's service, that we dare not under-
take with the assistance of His grace. I wish such
audacity to exist in this house – it increases
humility.

God aids the valiant and is 'no respecter of
persons'. Both to you and to me He will give the
help needed.

The prayer of quiet

However, if God sees that after He has set the kingdom of heaven within the soul, it turns to this world, not only will He desist from revealing to it the mysteries of His kingdom, but He will only show it the former favours at rare intervals and for a short time.

I believe that the reason why there are not more spiritual persons is that they do not respond worthily by their actions to this signal grace by preparing to receive it again.

As they withdraw from our Lord's hands their will, that He considered His property, and centre it on base things, He seeks other souls whose love for Him is so fervent that He can grant them even more sublime favours.

There are many souls who close their ears against Him because they prefer to speak and hurry through vocal prayers as if a task had been set them to say a certain amount everyday.

Do not imitate them. You are doing more by occasionally repeating a single petition of the Paternoster than by repeating the whole of it many times in a hurry and not thinking what you are saying.

The implications of giving our wills

When you say 'Thy will be done', you are begging that God's will may be carried out in you, for it is *this,* and nothing else, for which you ask.

You need not fear that He will give you riches or pleasures, or great honours, or any earthly good – His love for you is not so lukewarm. He places a higher value on your gift and wishes to reward you generously, since He gives you His kingdom even in this life.

Ask His glorious Son, Who in the garden uttered this petition truthfully and resolutely. See whether the will of God was not accomplished in the trials, sufferings, insults and persecutions sent Him, until at last his life was ended on the cross.

Thus you see what God gave to Him He loved best. I believe that our love is the measure of the cross, great or small, that we can bear.

Prayer in practice is love of one another

So far as you can without offending God, try to be genial and to behave in such a way with those you have to deal with that they may take pleasure in your conversation and may wish to imitate your life and manners, instead of being frightened and deterred from virtue.

The more holy someone is, the more cordial should they be with others.

Although you may be pained because their conversation is not what you would wish, never keep aloof if you want to help them and win their love.

Try to think rightly about God, sisters. He does not look at such trifling matters as you suppose; do not alarm your soul or lose courage for you might lose greatly. Keep a pure intention and a firm resolve not to offend God, as I said, but do not trammel your soul, for instead of advancing in sanctity you would contract a number of imperfections and would not help others as you might have done.

What

A Difference
Between
God's Will
And Ours

What a difference between God's will and ours

What a contrast there is between our will and God's will! His will is that we should love the truth, ours prefer falsehood. He wishes us to love what is eternal, we wish to follow what is fleeting. He wills us to care for the noble and sublime, we value only base and earthly things.

He wills that we desire only what is safe, we love danger. All things are vanity, save to ask God to deliver us from these dangers for ever and to preserve us now from all evil.

Although our wish for this may not be perfect let us force ourselves to make the petition, since we ask it of One Who is almighty. May His name be for ever blessed both in heaven and earth, and let His will be ever done in me. Amen.

Eucharist

 If, while Jesus lived in the world, the mere touch of His garments healed the sick, who can doubt that when He is dwelling in the very centre of our being He will work wonders of healing in us if we have a living faith in Him?

Will He not grant our petitions while He is our Guest? His Majesty is not a bad Paymaster for a good inn.

Are you grieved at not seeing Him with your bodily eyes? That would be a different matter now that He is glorified, from what it was when He lived in the world. Human nature would be too weak to bear it.

Beneath the accidents of bread, He is accessible – if the King disguises Himself, we can converse with Him without ceremonies and court etiquette: indeed He seems to have waived His claim to them by appearing incognito.

Take pleasure in remaining in His society: do not lose such precious time, for this hour is of the utmost value to the soul, and the good Jesus desires you to spend it with Him.

Stay with Him

When you have received our Lord, since He really dwells within you, try to close the eyes of your body and to open those of your soul; look into your heart.

I have told you, and shall tell you again and again, that if you accustom yourselves to keep with Him when you communicate, and if you strive to keep your conscience clear so that you may frequently enjoy this grace, His coming will not be so hidden but that, in many ways, He will reveal Himself to you, in proportion to the desire you have of seeing Him.

If we care nothing for Him but either go to seek Him elsewhere or busy ourselves about other and lower matters what would we have Him do? Must He drag us by force to look at Him and stay with Him?

He will not show Himself openly or reveal His glories or bestow His treasures, save on souls who prove that they ardently desire Him, for these are His real friends.

Forgive us as we forgive others

What value God places on our loving and keeping peace with one another! The good Jesus places it before anything else.

He could have said: 'Forgive us because of our many penances, and prayers and fasts, or because we have left all for Thee and love Thee fervently.' He never says 'Because we would lay down our lives for Thee', or recounts the many other things the soul does for God when it loves Him and gives Him its will. He only pleads: 'As we forgive our debtors.'

Perhaps this was because He knew of our attachment to our miserable 'honour', so that we will overlook no slight upon it. This being the most difficult thing for us to overcome, our Lord put it in the first place, so that, after having asked such sublime graces for us, He offers this to God on our part.

Notice that Christ says, 'As we have forgiven our debtors', to show that it is a thing we have already done.

True prayer results in ready forgiveness

I cannot believe that one who has approached so near to Mercy Himself, Who has shown the soul what it really is and all that God has pardoned it, would not instantly and most willingly forgive, and be at peace, and remain well-affected towards anyone who has injured her.

For the divine kindness and mercy shown her prove the immense love felt for her by the Almighty, and she is overjoyed at having an opportunity of showing love in return.

I repeat that I know a number of people whom our Lord has raised to supernatural things, giving them the prayer of contemplation I described, and though they have other faults and imperfections, I never saw one who was unforgiving, nor do I think it possible if these favours were from God.

God always enriches the souls He visits. This is certain, for although the favour and consolation may pass away quickly, it is detected later on by the benefits it has left in the soul.

Lead us not into temptation

Christ seems to have made a sort of agreement on our behalf with His eternal Father, as though to say: 'Do this, Lord, and my brethren will do that.'

It is very certain that He will not fail on His part. Oh, what a Paymaster He is and how limitless are His rewards!

Do not say one thing and mean another: if we treat Him with truth and candour, He always gives us more than we ask for.

Our Lord saw that it was necessary to arouse devout souls, and to remind them that they had enemies and that there is a special danger for them in growing careless. That they might also be guarded from being unwittingly deceived.

He offered these petitions, so necessary for all while we live in the exile of this world: 'Lead us not, Lord, into temptation, but deliver us from evil.'

A wound and a remedy

The evil one may secretly injure us seriously by making us believe that we have virtues which we do not possess – this is most pestilent.

In consolations and favours we seem only recipients and therefore feel the more strictly bound to serve God: but this delusion makes us think that we render Him some gift and service which He is called upon to repay.

By degrees this damages us greatly, for while on the one hand it weakens our humility, on the other we neglect to acquire the virtue we believe that we already own.

Suspecting no evil (for we think we are safe), we fall into a pit from which we cannot get out. So we are lamed, so that we cannot travel on the road I began to speak of. For how can anyone walk when he is plunged into a deep pit?

He can never make any progress and in any case can do nothing but harm to himself and others.

What remedy is there, sisters? That which our Master has taught us seems to me the best – to pray and beseech the eternal Father not to suffer us to fall into temptation.

The fact of self-deception

Let us now come to the time of trial – for we can only test ourselves by watching our actions narrowly, and we shall soon detect signs of deceptions.

For instance as regards humility. We fancy we do not wish for honour and that we are indifferent to everything of the kind – yet let anyone offer us the slightest affront, and our feelings and behaviour will at once betray that we are not humble.

Besides, if any opportunity occurs of augmenting our dignity we do not reject it for the sake of a greater good. And God grant we may not seek such honour.

We are so accustomed to saying that we want nothing and are indifferent to everything (which we really believe is the fact), that at last the very habit of asserting it convinces us of its truth more strongly.

It is wise to be aware that this is a temptation for when God gives us any solid virtue it brings all the others in its train.

When discouraged trust in God's mercy

Beware, daughters, of a certain kind of humility suggested by the devil which is accompanied by great anxiety about the gravity of our sins.

He disturbs souls in many ways by this means, until at last he stops them from receiving Holy Communion and from private prayer by doubts as to whether they are in a fit state for it, and such thoughts as: 'Am I worthy of it? Am I in a good disposition? I am unfit to live in a religious community.'

Thus Christians are hindered from prayer, and when they communicate, the time during which they ought to be obtaining graces is spent in wondering whether they are well prepared or no.

Everything such a person says seems to her on the verge of evil, and all her actions appear fruitless, however good they are in themselves. She becomes discouraged and unable to do any good, for what is right in others she fancies is wrong in herself.

When you are in this state, turn your mind so far as you can from your misery and fix it on the mercy of God, His love for us, and all that He suffered for our sake.

That feeling of security!

 Another very treacherous temptation is a feeling of security that we shall never relapse into our former faults or care for worldly pleasures again. We say to ourselves: 'Now I know what the world is, that all it contains passes away, and I care more for divine things.'

This temptation is the most dangerous of all, especially at the beginning of the religious life. Such souls, feeling safe, do not avoid customary occasions of sin which they enter blindfold, and God grant they may not fall lower than ever before, and that they may rise again. This the demon, seeing the harm they may do him and the good they may do their neighbour, will use every means in his power to prevent.

What, O eternal Father! can we do, except have recourse to Thee and beg Thee not to permit our enemies to lead us into temptation? You will be freed more quickly from temptation if you are near our Lord than if you were far off. Beg and entreat this freedom of Him, as you do every day in the Paternoster.

Strength

And

Safety
Lie In The
Love And
Fear Of God

Strength and safety lie in the love and fear of God

Give us, kind Master, some safeguard that we may live without overwhelming terror amid such perilous warfare.

The safeguards we may use, daughters, given us by His Majesty, are love and fear.

Love will make us quicken our steps and fear will lead us to look where we set our feet down lest we trip against the many stumbling blocks on the road by which all who live must travel. Thus armed, we shall be safe against deception.

The soul that truly loves God loves all good, seeks all good, protects all good, praises all good, joins itself to good men, helps and defends them, and embraces all the virtues: it only loves what is true and worth loving.

Do you think it possible that one who truly loves God cares, or can care, for vanities, or riches, or worldly things, or pleasures or honours? Neither can such a soul quarrel or feel envy, for it aims at nothing save pleasing its Beloved.

It dies with longing for His love and gives its life in striving how to please Him better.

The fear of God

The fear of God is easily recognized by its possessor and by those around her, although it develops gradually.

Whoever watches such persons narrowly will find that they are never careless, for God upholds them, so that, whatever they may gain by it, they would not willingly commit a venial fault – as for mortal sins, they dread them like fire.

Let us beg God that temptation may not be strong enough to overcome us, but that He will proportion it to the strength He will give us to overcome it (for it can do us little or no harm while we keep a good conscience). This is the fear which I hope we shall never lose: this must be our defence.

From wilfully committing any sin, however trivial, may God deliver us! Such a fault seems to be as if we said: 'Lord, although this displeases Thee, yet I shall do it. I know that Thou seest it and dost not wish it: this I understand, but I would rather follow my own fancies and desires than Thy will.'

Is such a misdeed as this a slight one? I think not: I consider it very, very serious however light the fault.

Deliver us from evil

Our good Master, knowing what the dangers and
trials of this life are, offered this petition for us,
but I think He might well have done so for
Himself, as we see how weary He was of this life
by His speech to His apostles at this supper: 'With
desire have I desired to eat this Pasch with you.'

As this was to be the last supper He ever ate, these
words prove how tired He was of living. Yet,
nowadays, people of a hundred years old, far from
being sick of existence, want to live longer!

But we do not dwell in such misery, sufferings,
and poverty as did His Majesty. What was His
whole life but a continuous death, with the cruel
end they were to give Him ever before His eyes?

Yet this was the least of His sorrows compared
with witnessing the sins committed against His
Father and the multitude of souls that are lost.

If this is a cruel torment to a heart filled with
charity, what must it have been to the boundless
and supreme charity of our Lord?

Take me where all good is found

I think that as 'Amen' comes at the end of all things, our Lord here means by it that we may be delivered from all evil for ever.

When I see how engulfed I am in my weakness, tepidity, lack of mortification, and many other faults, I feel the need to ask God for some remedy. Since I shall never be free from these evils in this life, I beg the Lord to deliver me from all evil for ever.

What good do we perceive on earth, where we are destitute of all good and absent from our Lord?

Deliver me, O God! from this deadly nightmare: from the many labours, the frequent anguish, the numberless vicissitudes, the multitude of duties, and the many, many, *many* things that harass and weary me.

Unbearable are the uncertainties as to whether I love Thee or whether my desires are pleasing to Thee. My Lord and my God! Deliver me from all evil and vouchsafe to take me where all good things are to be found.

Beware of flattery

Unless you are careful, praise from others may harm you greatly, for when once it begins it never ceases, and generally ends in running you down afterwards. This usually takes the form of telling you that you are more holy than others and such-like flattering speeches.

For the love of God, I implore you never to find your peace in such speeches for you might come to believe them, or to think you had done all you need and that your work was finished.

Remember how the world treated our Lord Jesus Christ, yet how it had extolled Him on Palm Sunday! Men so esteemed St John the Baptist as to mistake him for the Messiah, yet how barbarously and for what a motive they afterwards beheaded him!

Always struggle within your own heart against these dangerous flatteries, then you will go forth with deeper humility.

May God of His great bounty, give us light.

Proof of genuine prayer

When I see people very anxious to know what sort of prayer they practise, covering their faces and afraid to move or think, lest they should lose any slight tenderness and devotion they feel, I know how little they understand how to attain union with God, since they think it consists in such things as these.

No. Our Lord expects *works* from us!

If you see someone sick whom you can relieve, never fear losing your devotion; have compassion on her; if she is in pain, feel it as if it were your own, and, when there is need, fast so that she may eat, not so much for her sake as because you know your Lord asks it of you.

This is the true union of our will with the will of God.

If someone else is well spoken of, be more pleased than if it were yourself; this is easy enough, for if you were really humble it would vex you to be praised.

If you possess fraternal charity, I assure you that you will attain the union I have described.

Forget self-interest

 Beg our Lord to grant you perfect love for your neighbour and leave the rest to Him.

He will give you more than you know how to desire if you constrain yourselves and strive with all your power to gain it, forcing your will as far as possible to comply in all things with your sisters' wishes although you may sometimes forfeit your own rights by so doing. Forget your self-interests for theirs, however much nature may rebel: when opportunity occurs take some burden upon yourself to ease your neighbour of it.

Do not fancy that it will cost you nothing and that you will find it all done for you: think what the love He bore for us cost our Spouse, Who to free us from death Himself suffered the most painful death of all – the death of the cross.

God calls us to pray in different ways

Contemplation is a gift of God which is not necessary for salvation nor for earning our eternal reward, nor will anyone require you to possess it.

She who is without it, yet who follows the counsels I have given, will attain greater perfection. Rather she may gain more merit, as she has to work harder on her own account; our Lord is treating her like a valiant woman and keeping until hereafter all the happiness she has missed in this life.

Let her not be disheartened nor give up prayer for sometimes our Lord comes very late, and pays as much all at once as He has given to others during many years.

For more than fourteen years I could not even meditate without a book.

There are many people of this kind, and others cannot meditate even with the help of reading, but are obliged to recite vocal prayers, which to a certain extent arrest their attention.

Prayer and pride

I know a very old nun of most exemplary life in every way – would to God my life were like hers! – very holy, very austere, and a perfect religious, who has spent many hours for several years in vocal prayers, but cannot make use of mental prayer: the utmost she can do is to pause a little, from time to time (during her Ave Marias and Paternosters). Many people resemble her.

If they are humble, I do not think they are more imperfect or believe they will be any the worse for it in the end but quite as well off as those who enjoy many consolations.

In one way such souls are safer, for we cannot tell whether spiritual delights come from God or from the devil: if they are not divine they are very dangerous, for Satan tries to excite pride by their means: however, if they are sent by God there is nothing to fear for they bring humility with them.

On to the fountain of living water

Now you see, friends, that to make vocal prayer perfectly is to consider and realize from Whom we ask, who it is who asks, and what we ask.

Do not be disheartened if people tell you that it is wrong to use any but vocal prayer. Beg God to teach you anything about the subject that you cannot understand. Nobody can hinder you from vocal prayer nor force you to say the Paternoster hurriedly and thoughtlessly.

If anyone tries to prevent your prayer or advises you to give it up, do not trust what he says but look upon him as a false prophet. In these times you must not listen to everybody: if today someone tells you that you have nothing to fear, there is no knowing what he may say tomorrow.

To know how to recite the Paternoster well will show you how to say all other prayers.

As you have seen: it comprises the whole spiritual life from the very beginning until God absorbs the soul into Himself and gives it to drink freely of the fountain of living water which I told you was to be found at the end of the way.

Sources and Index

I have used David Lewis' translation of *The Life of St Teresa of Jesus*, edited by Benedict Zimmerman OCD (1910); and the translations by the Benedictines of Stanbrook of *The Interior Castle* (1912), *Conceptions of the Love of God* and *Exclamations* from the *Minor Works* (1913), and *The Way of Perfection* (1935).

I have taken the liberty of omitting phrases, or even paragraphs, and combining passages so as to achieve a greater concentration of St Teresa's teaching.

There are many commentaries on St Teresa but *Saint Teresa of Avila* by Marcelle Auclair is a most readable biography and a small Dominican pamphlet in their RLR Series 3 is very informative (obtainable 69 Upper O'Connell Street, Dublin 1).